CW00517201

150 Most ~~Beau~~ French Quotes

Translated into English

Valerie Pollmann R.

Introduction

There is something very special about the so called "language of love". A language that you can hear in all five continents. It is one of the very few languages spoken all over the world, ranked as the sixth most widely spoken language after Mandarin Chinese, English, Hindi, Spanish and Arabic. It is said that there are currently over 220 million French speakers worldwide and it is believed that one in three English words derive directly from French.

My love for quotes and my passion for languages inspired me to write this book. A personal selection of my favorite quotes by French authors, actors, philosophers, politicians, songwriters, poets and many more, for everyone that loves French, is learning French, wants to learn French, translated into English.

About Love

"Il n'est rien de reel que le rêve et l'amour"

-

Nothing is real but dream and love
— *Anna de Noailles*

"L'amour est une passion qui ne se soumet à rien, et à qui au contraire, toutes choses se soumettent"

-

Love is a passion which surrenders to nothing, but to the contrary, everything surrenders to love
— *Madeleine de Scudéry*

"Le prix d'Amour, c'est seulement Amour... Il faut aimer si l'on veut etre aimé..."

-

The price of love is love itself… One must love if one wants to be loved...
— *Honoré d'Urfé*

"Une historie d'amour c'est les bonnes personnes au bon moment. Mais souvent dans la vie, c'est les bonnes personnes mais pas au bon moment; et puis un jour, le moment revient.."

-

A love story is the right person at the right time. But often in life, it's the right person but not at the right time; and then one day, the moment comes back…
— *Marc Lévy*

"L'amour est l'emblème de l'éternité, il confound toute la notion de temps, efface toute la mémoire d'un commencement, toute la crainte d'une extrémité"

-

Love is the emblem of eternity, it confounds all notion of time, effaces all memory of a beginning, all fear of an end

— *Madame de Staël*

"J'ai aimé jusqu'à atteindre la folie. Ce que certains appellent la folie, mais ce qui pour moi, est la seule façon d'aimer"

-

I have loved to the point of madness. That which is called madness, that which to me, is the only sensible way to love

— *Françoise Sagan*

"L'amour représente toute ce qu'il est nécessaire de savoir et de retenir. Il n'y a rien d'autre à apprendre. Celui qui sait cela, sait tout"

-

Love is all that is necessary to know and hold, there is nothing else to learn, whoever knows that, knows everything

—— *Vladimir Jankélévitch*

"Les raisons d'aimer et de vivre varient comme font les saisons"

-

The reasons to love and live vary as the seasons do

—— *Louis Aragon*

"Rien n'est plus important que d'aimer"

-

Nothing is more important than to love

—— *Jacques Attali*

"L'amour est la poésie den sens"

-

Love is the poetry of the senses
— *Balzac*

"On ne peut aimer que si l'on est ivre de vie"

-

One can only love if one is drunk with life
— *Tahar Ben Jelloun*

"Ce qui ressemble à l'amour est toujours de l'amour"

-

What looks like love is always love
— *Tristan Bernard*

"L'homme commence par aimer l'amour et finit par aimer une femme. La femme commence par aimer un homme et finit par aimer l'amour"

-

Man begins by loving love and ends up loving a woman. Woman begins by loving a man and ends up loving love

— *Remy de Gourmont*

"Elle répétait que l'amour véritable n'est pas dans les commencements, qui se ressemblent tous, mais dans l'élaboration lente d'un lien particulier"

-

She reiterated that true love is not in the beginnings, which are all alike, but in the slow elaboration of a particular bond

— *Alexandre Jardin*

"Aimer est une aventure sans carte et sans compas où seule la prudence égare"

-

To love is an adventure without a map and without a compass where only prudence is misguided
— *Romain Gary*

"Nous n'avons besoin de morale que faute d'amour"

-

We need morality only because we do not have enough love
— *André Comte-Sponville*

"Les femmes vivent plus longtemps que les hommes. Surtout quand elles sont veuves"

-

Women live longer than men, especially when they are widowed
— *Georges Clemenceau*

"À cœur vaillant, rien d'impossible"

-

For a valiant heart, nothing is impossible
Jacques Cœur

"C'est une folie de hair toutes les roses parce qu'une épine vous a piqué"

-

It is madness to hate all roses because you were stung by one thorn
— Antoine de Saint-Exupéry

"J'accepte la grande aventure d'etre moi"

-

I accept the great adventure of being me
— Simon de Beauvoir

"Le baiser est la plus sûre façon de se taire en disant tout"

-

A kiss is the surest way to quite oneself while saying everything

— *Guy de Maupassant*

About Life

"Si la vie n'est qu'un passage, sur ce passage au moins semons des fleurs"

-

If life is nothing more than a passage, let's at least sow flowers along it

— *Michel de Montaigne*

"Une forme de générosité consisterait à s'émerveiller du cadeau que représente le seul fait d'exister à chaque instant de la vie"

-

A form of generosity would be to marvel at the gift of being there every moment of life

— *Jacques Salomé*

"Je suis l'homme de ma vie"

-

I am the man of my life
— *Brigitte Bardot*

"La vie a beaucoup plus d'imagination que nous"

-

Life has a lot more imagination than us
— *François Truffaut*

"Plus tard ce sera trop tard. Notre vie c'est maintenant"

-

Later it will be too late. Our life is now
— *Jacques Prévert*

"Ce n'est pas parce que la vie n'est pas élégante qu'il faut se
conduire comme elle"

-

Just because life isn't elegant doesn't mean you shouldn't be
— *Françoise Sagan*

"L'enfance, c'est le moment le plus intense de la vie"

-

Childhood is the most intense moment of life
— *Jacques-Yves Cousteau*

"L'aventure est un état d'esprit. Elle se trouve dans le cœur
de l'homme. L'aventure, c'est être capable de refuser son
destin, être prêt à partir à tout moment, concevoir encore et
toujours de nouveaux projets, ne pas être assis, c'est en un
mot vivre sa vie et la construiré"

-

Adventure is a state of mind, it is in the heart of man,
adventure is to be able to refuse one's destiny, to be ready to
leave at any moment, to conceive again and again new
projects, not to be seated, it is in a word to live one's life and
to build it
— *Paul-Émile Victor*

"Il n'y a qu'une vie, c'est donc qu'elle est parfait"

-

There is only one life, therefore it is perfect
— *Paul Éluard*

"Abandonne ce qui ne t'appartient plus, abandonne ce qui ne t'appartient pas, reprends les rênes de ta vie; reprends ton plein pouvoir, tu verras c'est magique"

-

Abandon what does not belong to you anymore, give up what does not belong to you, take back the reins of your life; take back your full power, you'll see its magic

— *Karine Besseau*

"Fais que chaque heure de ta vie soit belle. Le moindre geste est un souvenir futur"

-

Make every hour of your life beautiful, the slightest gesture is a future memory

— *Claude Aveline*

"Vivre, c'est faire de son rêve un souvenir"

-

To live is to make a memory out of one's dream
— *Sylvain Tesson*

"La Misère est le manque du nécessaire, la Pauvreté est le
manque du superflu"

-

Misery is the lack of the necessary, Poverty is the lack of the
superfluous
— *León Bloy*

"Je vous souhaite des rêves à n'en plus finir, et l'envie furieuse
d'en réaliser quelques uns"

-

I wish for you to have endless dreams and the furious desire to
achieve some of them
— *Jacques Brel*

"Il faut faire aujourd'hui ce que tout le monde fera demain"

-

Do today what everyone else will do tomorrow
— *Jean Cocteau*

"Le seul péché est de ne pas se risquer pour vivre son désir"

-

The only sin is not to risk oneself to live one's desire
— *Françoise Dolto*

"Gardez bien en vous ce trésor, la gentillesse. Sachez donner sans retenue, perdre sans regret, acquérir sans mesquinerie"

-

Guard well within you this treasure, kindness. Know how to give without hesitation, how to loose without regret, how to acquire without meanness
— *George Sand*

"La mort, c'est comme un bateau qui s'éloigne vers l'horizon. Il y a un moment où il disparaît. Mais ce n'est pas parce qu'on ne le voit plus qu'il n'existe plus"

-

Death is like a boat going off to the horizon, there is a moment when it disappears, but it's not because we no longer see it that it no longer exists
— *Marie de Hennezel*

"Partir, c'est mourir un peu. Mais mourir, c'est partir beaucoup"

-

To leave is to die a little, but to die is to leave a lot
— *Alphonse Allais*

"Il n'est rien de plus précieux que le temps, puisque c'est le prix de l'éternité"

-

There is nothing more precious than time, since it is the price of eternity

— *Louis Bourdaloue*

"L'expérience de chacun est le trésor de tous"

-

Everyone's experience is everyone's treasure

— *Gérard de Nerval*

About Travels

"Rester, c'est exister. Mais voyager, c'est vivre"

-

To stay in the same place is to exist. But to travel is to live
— *Gustave Nadaud*

"Cela rend modeste de voyager. On voit quelle petite place on occupe dans le monde"

-

Traveling makes you humble. You see what a tiny place you occupy in the world
— *Gustave Flaubert*

"Le monde est livre et ceux qui ne voyagent pas n'en lisent qu'une page"

-

The world is a book and those who do not travel read only one page
— *Saint Augustin*

"Je ne sais où va mon chemin mais je marche mieux quand ma main serre la tienne"

-

I don't know where my road is going but I know that I walk better when I hold your hand
— *Alfred de Musset*

"La liberté consiste à faire tout ce que permet la longueur de la chaîne"

-

Freedom is about doing everything the length of the chain allows

— *François Cavanna*

About Happiness

"Rien n'empêche le bonheur comme le souvenir du bonheur"

-

Nothing prevents happiness as the memory of happiness

— *André Gide*

"Un grand obstacle au bonheur, c'est de s'attendre à un trop grand Bonheur"

-

A big obstacle to happiness is to expect too much happiness

— *Bernard Fontenelle*

"Le Bonheur est parfois cache dans l'inconnu"

-

Happiness is sometimes hidden in the unknown

— *Victor Hugo*

"La mer imite le bruit du Bonheur"

-

The sea imitates the sound of happiness
— *Régis Jauffret*

"Impose ta chance, serre ton bonheur et va vers tes risques.
A te regarder, ils s'habitueront"

-

Impose your luck, squeeze your happiness and go to your
risks. To look at you, they will get used to it
— *René Char*

"Le bonheur est toujours une quête à renouveler"

-

Happiness is always a quest to renew
— *Michel Piccoli*

"Le Bonheur le plus doux est celui qu'on partage"

-

The sweetest happiness is the one that we share
— *Jacques Delille*

"Le Bonheur est souvent la seule chose qu'on puisse donner
sans l'avoir et c'est en le donnant qu'on l'acquiert"

-

Happiness often is the only thing we can give without having
it, and we get it when we give it
— *Volatire*

"Je crois que tout malheur ne vient que d'erreurs et que tout bonheur nous est procuré par la vérité; faisons donc tous nos efforts pour connaître cette vérité"

-

I believe that all misfortune comes only from errors and that all happiness is procured by the truth, so let us make every effort to know this truth

— *Stendhal*

"Il ne faut pas avoir peur du bonheur. C'est seulement un bon moment à passer"

-

You should not be afraid of the happiness. It is only a good moment to pass

— *Romain Gary*

"Heureux soient les fêlés, car ils laisseront passer la lumière"

-

Happy are the cracked ones, for they will let the light through

— *Michel Audiard*

About Beauty

"Le beau est toujours bizarre"

-

The beautiful is always bizarre
— *Charles Baudelaire*

"Et nous avons des nuits plus belles que vos jours"

-

And we have nights that are more beautiful than your days
— *Racine*

"Une belle femme plaît aux yeux, une bonne femme plaît au coeur; l'une est un bijou, l'autre un trésor"

-

A beautiful woman pleases the eyes, a good woman pleases the heart; one is a jewel, the other a treasure
— *Napoleon Bonaparte*

"La beauté commence au moment où vus décidez d'être vous-même"

-

Beauty begins the moment you decide to be yourself

— *Coco Chanel*

"Sans élégance de cœur, il n'y a pas d'élégance"

-

Without elegance of heart, there is no elegance

— *Yves Saint Laurent*

"Il y a des fleurs partout pour qui veut bien les voir"

-

There are flowers everywhere for who wants to see them

— *Henri Matisse*

"Toute chose appartient à qui sait en jouir"

-

Everything belongs to those who can appreciate it
— *André Gide*

"La vanité est la passion dominante de l'homme"

-

Vanity is the dominant passion of man

— *Henry de Montherlant*

"La grâce entoure l'élégance, et la revêt"

-

Grace surrounds elegance, and dresses it
— *Joseph Joubert*

About Knowledge

"Avoir une autre langue, c'est posséder une deuxième âme"

-

To have another language is to possess a second soul
— *Charlemagne*

"Je connais mes limites. C'est pourquoi je vais au-delà"

-

I know my limits. That's why I go beyond them
— *Serge Gainsbourg*

"Je lis pour m'enfuir, j'écris pour revenir"

-

I read to escape, I write to return
— *Frédéric Beigbeder*

"Laissez lire, et laissez danser; ces deux amusements ne feront jamais de mal au monde"

-

Let us read, and let us dance; these two amusements will never do the world any harm
— *Volatire*

"Je crois à l'immortalité. Et pourtant je crains bien de mourir avant de la connaître"

-

I believe in immortality, and yet I'm afraid I'll die before I know it
— *Raymon Devos*

"L'homme aimable est celui qui écoute en souriant les choses
qu'il sait dites par quelqu'un qui les ignore"

-

The kind man is the one who listens smilingly to the things
he knows by someone who ignores them
— *Alfred Capus*

"La grandeur est un chemin vers quelque chose qu'on ne
connaît pas"

-

Greatness is a way to something we do not know
— *Charles de Gaulle*

"Tout vient à point à qui sait attendre"

-

Good things come to those who wait
— *Clément Marot*

"Retrouver la fraîcheur du regard, oublier ce que l'on croit savoir, se tenir devant les êtres et les choses comme si on les voyait pour la première fois"

-

Recover the freshness of the eyes, forget what you think you know, stand before people and things as if you saw them for the first time
— *André Frossard*

"Je me suis souvent repenti d'avoir parlé, mais jamais de m'être tu"

-

I have often repented for speaking, but never for staying silent
— *Philippe de Commynes*

"Quand un philosophe me répond, je ne comprends plus ma question"

-

When a philosopher answers me, I do not understand my question anymore
— *Pierre Desproges*

"Pourquoi les enfants étant si intelligents, les hommes sont-ils si bêtes? Cela doit tenir à l'éducation"

-

How is it that little children are so intelligent and men so stupid? It must be education that does it
— *Alexandre Dumas, fils*

"Ce qu'on apprend au milieu des fléaux cést qu'il y a chez l'homme plus de choses à admirer qu'à mépriser"

-

What we learn in the midst of plagues is that there are more things to admire in men than there are to despise

— *Albert Camus*

"Si tous ceux qui croient avoir raison n'avaient pas tort, la vérité ne serait pas loin"

-

If all who believe they are right were not wrong, the truth would not be far

— *Pierre Dac*

"La science est l'esthétique de l'intelligence"

-

Science is the aesthetics of intelligence

— *Gaston Bachelard*

"Qui ôte à l'esprit la réflexion lui ôte toute sa force"

-

Whoever removes thought from his mind takes away all his
strength
— *Jacques-Bénigne Boussuet*

"La vérité existe; on n'invente que le mensonge"

-

The truth exists, we only invent the lie
— *Georges Braque*

"Ayez le culte de l'esprit critique"

-

Have a cult of critical thinking
— *Louis Pasteur*

"Rien ne pèse tant qu'un secret"

-

Nothing weighs more than a secret
— *Jean de La Fontaine*

"La méditation, c'est une sorte d'entraînement à pactiser avec
notre esprit"

-

Meditation, it's a kind of training to make a deal with our
spirit
— *Christophe André*

"La mémoire a pour but de triompher de l'absence et c'est
cette lutte contre l'absence qui caractérise la mémoire"

-

The purpose of memory is to overcome absence, and it is
this struggle against absence that characterizes memory
— *Pierre Janet*

About Human Beings

"Chaque homme est une histoire qui n'est identique à aucune autre"

-

Every man is a story that is not identical to any other
— *Alexis Carrel*

"...La vraie puissance d'un homme est conditionnée à l'acceptation de sa vulnérabilité"

-

... The true power of a man is conditioned to acceptance of its vulnerability
— *Jacques Lucas*

"Nous ne sommes pas des êtres humains ayant une expérience spirituelle. Nous sommes des êtres spirituels ayant une expérience humaine"

-

We are not human beings with spiritual experience. We are spiritual beings with a human experience
— *Pierre Teilhard de Chardin*

"Les hommes croient choisir leur femme: c'est toujours la femme qui harponne"

-

Men believe they choose their wife: it is always the woman who harpoon
— *René Barjavel*

"L'homme est né libre et partout il est dans les fers"

-

Man is born free and everywhere he is in chains
— *Jean-Jacques Rousseau*

"Les humains sont comparables à celui qui serait plongé dans un lac et qui crierait: "De l'eau, de l'eau, j'ai soif !"". Ils sont plongés dans l'océan de la lumière cosmique, mais ils ont de telles carapaces que cette lumière ne peut pas pénétrer en eux"

-

Humans are like the one who would be plunged into a lake and shout: "Water, water, I'm thirsty!" They are immersed in the ocean of cosmic light, but they have such shells as this light cannot penetrate into them.
— *Aïvanhov (Omraam Mikhaël)*

"La révolte, c'est le moment où l'on ressent la honte d'être un homme"

-

Revolt is the moment when one feels the shame of being a man
— *Gilles Deleuze*

"C'est drôle ce besoin qu'ont les gens d'accuser les autres d'avoir gâché leur existence. Alors qu'ils y parviennent si bien eux-mêmes, sans l'aide de quiconque"

-

It's funny that people need to blame others for ruining their lives, and that they do it so well without the help of anyone
— *Amélie Nothomb*

"¡Si vous compreniez à quel point l'ignorance humaine conduit la Terre à sa destruction, vous en seriez terrifié!"

-

If you understand how human ignorance leads the Earth to its destruction, you would be terrified!
— *Françoise Giroud*

"L'humour ne peut exister que là où les gens discernent encore la frontière entre ce qui important et ce qui ne l'est pas"

-

Humor can exist only where people still discern the boundary between what is important and what is not
— *Milan Kundera*

"Les gens prudents sont des infirmes"

-

Cautious people are disabled
Jacques Brel

"On vit dans un monde de karaoké où les gens répètent les mots des autres"

-

We live in a world of karaoke where people repeat the words of others
— *Anonyme*

"Le silence des peuples est la leçon des rois"

-

The silence of the people is the lesson of kings
— *Comte de Mirabeau*

"Regarde où l'ennemi t'attaque: c'est souvent son propre
point faible"

-

Look where the enemy is attacking you: it's often his own
weak point
— *Bernard Werber*

"N'importe quel peuple, à un certain moment de sa carrière, se croit élu. C'est alors qu'il donne le meilleur et le pire de lui-même"

-

Any person, at a certain moment of their career, think themselves elected. It is then that he shows the best and the worst of himself

— *Emil Cioran*

"Qui exagère ses bonnes qualités en ôte le mérite par son orgueil"

-

Whoever exaggerates his good qualities, takes away his merit by his pride

— *Antoine Gombaud*

"Pour avoir du talent, il faut être convaincu qu'on en possède"

-

To be talented, you have to be convinced that you have some

— *Gustave Flaubert*

"Dis-moi qui tu admires et je te dirai qui tu es"

-

Tell me who you admire and I will tell you who you are

— *Charles-Augustin Sainte-Beuve*

"Personne n'est sujet a plus de fautes que ceux qui n'agissent que par réflexion"

-

— No one is subject to more faults than those who act only by reflection

— *Vauvenargues*

"Le fâcheux avec les hommes, c'est qu'ils vous déçoivent toujours, soit qu'on s'y fie, soit qu'on s'en méfie"

-

The trouble with men is that they always disappoint you, whether you trust it or be wary of it

— *Élie Fréron*

Miscellaneous

"A vaincre sans péril, on triomphe sans gloire"

-

To win without risk is a triumph without glory

— *Corneille*

"Il viendra un jour un être au regard si vrai que le réel le suivra"

-

One day there will be a being with a look so true that the real will follow him

— *Joë Bousquet*

"Le premier pas pour avoir ce que vous voulez, c'est d'avoir le courage de quitter ce que vous ne voulez plus"

-

The first step to having what you want is to have the courage to leave what you do not want anymore

— *Anonyme*

"L'idéologie est toujours l'idéologie de l'autre"

-

Ideology is always the ideology of the other

— *Raymond Claude Ferdinand Aron*

"Quand le chat n'est pas là les souris dansent"

-

When the cat is away, the mice dance

— *Inconnu / Unknown*

"Je ne crois en rien, ou presque. Je crois en moi, ce qui n'est déjà pas mal"

-

I do not believe in anything, or almost, I believe in myself, which is not bad
— *Jean Yanne*

"La bonne musique ne se trompe pas, et va droit au fond de l'âme chercher le chagrin qui nous dévore"

-

The good music is not mistaken, and goes straight to the bottom of the soul to seek the sorrow that devours us
— *Stendhal*

"Bien au-delà des plaisirs superficiels toujours inassouvis, la sobriété permet de retrouver la vibration de l'enchantement, le sentiment de ces êtres premiers pour qui la création, les créatures et la terre étaient avant tout sacrées"

-

Well beyond the superficial pleasures always unsatisfied, sobriety allows to find the vibration of enchantment, the feeling of those first beings for whom creation, creatures and the earth were above all sacred

— *Pierre Rabhi*

"Toutes les inventions des hommes ne sont que des imitations assez grossières de ce que la nature exécute avec la dernière perfection"

-

All the inventions of men are only gross imitations of what nature does with the utmost perfection

— *Georges-Louis Leclerc, comte de Buffon*

"Pleure: les larmes sont les petals de cœur"

-

Cry: tears are the hearts petals
— *Paul Éluard*

"La terre est devenue trop petite pour la méchanceté des hommes"

-

The earth has become too small for the wickedness of men
— *Maurice Chapelan*

"Le temps est un grand maître, dit-on. Le malheur est qu'il tue ses élèves"

-

Time is a great master, it is said, and the misfortune is that he kills his pupils.
— *Hector Beriloz*

"La douleur qui se tait n'en est que plus funeste"

-

The pain that is silent is all the more fatal
— *Jean Racine*

"En affaires, mentir n'est jamais nécessaire, rarement utile et
toujours dangereux"

-

In business, lying is never necessary, rarely useful and always
dangerous
— *Auguste Detoeuf*

"L'ennui est entré dans le monde par la paresse"

-

Boredom entered the world by laziness
— *Jean de la Bruyère*

"La meilleure façon de réaliser ses rêves est de se réveiller"

-

The best way to make your dreams come true is to wake up
— *Paul Valéry*

"Ce qu'il faut, c'est devenir soi-même une source de bien-
être. Voyez le soleil, il est le soleil, il ne peut pas s'empêcher de
répandre de la chaleur et de la lumière"

-

What is needed is to become a source of well-being. See the
sun, it's the sun, it cannot help but spread heat and light
— *Alexandra David-Néel*

"Il est plus facile à l'imagination de se composer un enfer
avec la douleur, qu'un paradis avec le plaisir"

-

It is easier for the imagination to compose a hell with pain,
than a paradise with pleasure
— *Antoine de Rivarol*

"La confiance est à la fois un élan spontané, sans condition ni certitude, et un défi au long cours, qui appelle sans cesse une mise à l'épreuve"

-

Confidence is both a spontaneous, unconditional, and uncertain impulse, and a long-term challenge, one that continually calls for a test
— *Jean Birnbaum*

"On ne fait jamais attention à ce qui a été fait; on ne voit que ce qui reste à faire"

-

We never pay attention to what has been done, we only see what remains to be done
— *Marie Curie*

"Un auteur doit être dans un livre comme la police dans la ville: partout et nulle part"

-

An author must be in a book like the police in the city: everywhere and nowhere
— *Edmond Huot de Goncourt*

"Qui craint de souffrir, il souffre déjà de ce qu'il craint"

-

He who fears suffering is already suffering that which he fears
— *La Fontaine*

"L'optimisme n'est pas une solution de facilité, mais un stimulant"

-

Optimism is not a solution of ease, but a stimulant
— *Jean Cazeneuve*

"Dès que l'on descend dans l'inconscient, l'émotion naît. Et le cinéma ne devrait être qu'un montage d'émotions"

-

As soon as we fall in the unconscious, the emotion is born. And the cinema should only be a montage of emotions

— *Alain Resnais*

"Le désir s'exprime par la caresse comme la pensée par le langage"

-

Desire is expressed by touch as thought is expressed by language

— *Jean-Paul Sartre*

"Écrire, c'est une façon de parler sans être interrompu"

-

Writing is a way to talk without being interrupted

— *Jules Renard*

Hope you enjoyed these quotes and learned a little French while reading this book. Would love to hear about your favorite ones in a review on Amazon.

Printed in Great Britain
by Amazon

80544984R00036